Table of Contents

Who Was Ruth Bader Ginsburg?   4

Growing Up in Brooklyn   8

Working Hard   12

Ginsburg's Cool Firsts   20

Back to the Big City   22

Fighting for Equality   26

6 Cool Facts About Ginsburg   34

Supreme Court   36

Lasting Legacy   42

Quiz Whiz   44

Glossary   46

Index   48

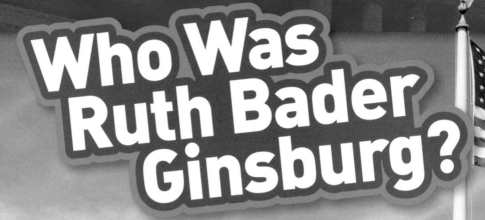

Who Was Ruth Bader Ginsburg?

Ruth Bader Ginsburg is best known for being a justice, or judge, on the United States Supreme Court. She was the second woman in history to have this job.

Ruth Bader Ginsburg

Rose Davidson

**NATIONAL
GEOGRAPHIC**

Washington, D.C.

For all the fierce women in my life —R.D.

Published by National Geographic Partners, LLC, Washington, DC 20036.

Designed by Yay! Design

The author and publisher gratefully acknowledge the fact-checking review of this book by Robin Palmer, as well as the literacy review of this book by Mariam Jean Dreher, professor of reading education, University of Maryland, College Park.

Trade paperback ISBN: 978-1-4263-3997-4
Reinforced library binding ISBN: 978-1-4263-3998-1

Photo Credits

AL=Alamy Stock Photo; AS=Adobe Stock; GI=Getty Images; SS=Shutterstock
Cover, Collection of the Supreme Court of the United States/Tribune News Service via GI; cover (background), Bob Pool/SS; top border (throughout), Gary Blakeley/SS; vocabulary art (throughout), Stanislav Novoselov/SS; 1, Timothy Greenfield-Sanders/Contour RA by GI; 3, graphixmania/SS; 4, Stringer/GI; 4-5, Orhan Cam/SS; 6, Doug Mills/AP/SS; 7, Librado Romero/The New York Times/Redux Pictures; 8, Hulton Archive/GI; 9, Anthony Potter Collection/GI; 10, Universal History Archive/Universal Images Group via GI; 11 (UP), Doug Mills/AP/SS; 11 (LO), AztecBlue/AL; 12, Collection of the Supreme Court of the United States; 13, haveseen/AS; 14, Collection of the Supreme Court of the United States; 15, jStock/AS; 16 (UP), WavebreakMediaMicro/AS; 16 (LO), Nikki Kahn/ The Washington Post via GI; 17, Brooks Kraft LLC/Corbis via GI; 18, Collection of the Supreme Court of the United States; 19, Louis Russo/The Boston Globe via GI; 20, Nikki Kahn/The Washington Post via GI; 21 (UP), pixelrobot/AS; 21 (CTR), courtesy Columbia Law School; 21 (LO), Maurice Savage/AL; 22-23, Barry Winiker/GI; 24, Benjamin Clapp/SS; 25, courtesy Rutgers Law School, Newark; 26, courtesy Columbia University; 27, Clare Cushman; 28, Lynn Gilbert; 29, Collection of the Supreme Court of the United States; 30, Collection of the Supreme Court of the United States; 31, stock_photo_world/SS; 32, Universal History Archive/UIG/SS; 34 (UP), Stephen R Brown/AP/SS; 34 (CTR), Collection of the Supreme Court of the United States; 34 (LO), Ilya S. Savenok/ GI for Berggruen Institute; 35 (UP), Collection of the Supreme Court of the United States; 35 (CTR), iMAGINE/AS; 35 (LO), TCD/Prod.DB/AL; 36, David Ake/AFP via GI; 37, Marcy Nighswander/AP/SS; 38, Patrick Fraser/Corbis via GI; 39 (UP RT), Chip Somodevilla/GI; 39 (CTR LE), Hilary Andrews/NG Staff; 39 (LO RT), WDC Photos/AL; 40-43 (skyline: Supreme Court building), filo/GI; 40-43 (skyline: all other buildings), greens87/AS; 41 (UP), Kevin Dietsch/ UPI Photo/AL; 41 (CTR), Doug Mills/AP/SS; 42, Pablo Martinez Monsivais-Pool/GI; 44 (UP), Steve Petteway/ AL; 44 (CTR), courtesy Rutgers Law School, Newark; 44 (LO), Stefan/AS; 45 (UP LE), stock_photo_world/ SS; 45 (UP RT), Hilary Andrews/NG Staff; 45 (LO LE), Anthony Potter Collection/GI; 45 (LO RT), Jack Vartoogian/GI; 46 (UP), Andrey_Popov/SS; 46 (CTR LE), 210484kate/AS; 46 (CTR RT), Orhan Cam/SS; 46 (LO LE), mast3r/AS; 46 (LO RT), courtesy Columbia Law School; 47 (UP LE), Marcy Nighswander/AP/ SS; 47 (UP RT), ink drop/AS; 47 (CTR LE), Hermann Mueller/GI; 47 (CTR RT), Prostock-studio/AS; 47 (LO LE), zimmytws/GI; 47 (LO RT), Orhan Cam/SS

Printed in the United States of America
20/WOR/1

The Supreme Court has an important role. The nine justices on the Court have the final say on how laws should be followed. Their decisions can help shape new laws.

the Supreme Court building

Word to Know

SUPREME COURT: The highest court of law in the United States

Before becoming a justice, Ginsburg was a professor and a lawyer. She helped people understand the law. She saw that people were not always treated equally. Sometimes women were not allowed to do or have the same things as men.

Ginsburg felt all people should have equality. In her work, she fought for laws that would give women equal treatment. By standing up and speaking out, she won important cases for women's rights.

In 1993, Ginsburg became the 107th justice to serve on the U.S. Supreme Court.

Ginsburg in 1972

Words to Know

PROFESSOR: A teacher at a college or university

EQUALITY: The same treatment and opportunities as others

Growing Up in Brooklyn

Ginsburg was born Joan Ruth Bader. She was born on March 15, 1933, in Brooklyn, New York, U.S.A. When she was

the Brooklyn Bridge and New York City around 1930

in kindergarten, other girls in her class were named Joan, too. So she started going by Ruth instead.

Ruth's family was Jewish. While traveling on a family vacation in Pennsylvania, U.S.A., Ruth saw prejudice against Jewish people. A sign said that no Jews were allowed. But she saw prejudice in her own neighborhood, too. Throughout her life, she remembered how this prejudice made her feel.

A Painful Past

Ruth grew up during World War II, which took place from 1939 to 1945. In the United States, Jewish people often experienced prejudice. But in many parts of Europe, Jewish people faced great danger. At that time, Germany was under the control of Adolf Hitler and his political group, the Nazis (NOT-sees). During the war, they took their hatred of Jewish people to an extreme. In a terrible event called the Holocaust (HOL-uh-kost), the Nazis killed six million Jewish people throughout Europe.

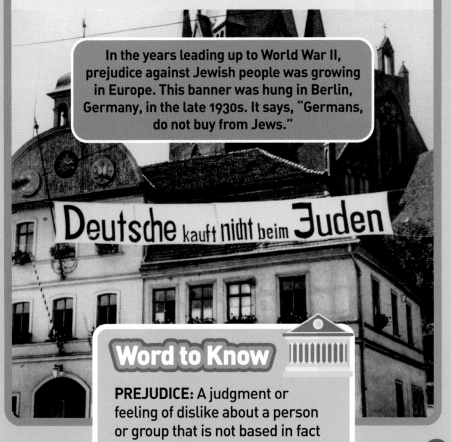

In the years leading up to World War II, prejudice against Jewish people was growing in Europe. This banner was hung in Berlin, Germany, in the late 1930s. It says, "Germans, do not buy from Jews."

Word to Know

PREJUDICE: A judgment or feeling of dislike about a person or group that is not based in fact

Ruth spent many hours reading at one of the public libraries in Brooklyn.

Ruth's parents didn't go to college, but they taught her that education was important. Her mother often took her to the library. There, Ruth discovered a love for reading and learning.

When Ruth was in high school, her mother got sick with cancer. She died two days before Ruth graduated. Remembering what her mother had taught her, Ruth wanted to keep learning.

That's a FACT! Growing up, Ruth loved reading the Nancy Drew detective series.

Working Hard

Ruth in 1953, when she was a student at Cornell

After high school, Ruth went to Cornell University in Ithaca (ITH-uh-kuh), New York. She got a scholarship to study government. In her classes, she learned how countries, states, and cities are run.

Cornell University

During her first year of college, Ruth met a student named Marty Ginsburg. He and Ruth were very different. Marty was outgoing and funny. Ruth was quiet and serious. But they liked each other. Soon they started dating.

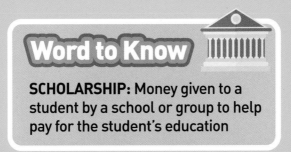

Word to Know

SCHOLARSHIP: Money given to a student by a school or group to help pay for the student's education

In 1954, Ruth graduated from Cornell. Nine days later, she married Marty and became

Marty and Ruth, celebrating their upcoming wedding

Ruth Bader Ginsburg. Marty was a year older and had already started studying at Harvard Law School in Massachusetts, U.S.A. But then he was drafted into the Army and was sent to Oklahoma, U.S.A. Ginsburg and Marty spent two years there and had a daughter named Jane.

After the Army, Marty went back to his studies at Harvard. Ginsburg was ready for a new challenge, too. She liked to write and solve problems. Her professors had encouraged her to become a lawyer. To do that, she needed to go to law school. She went to study at Harvard, too.

Harvard Law School

In Her Own Words

"Reading is the key that opens doors to many good things in life. Reading shaped my dreams, and more reading helped me make my dreams come true."

At Harvard, there were more than 500 people in Ginsburg's law school class. But there were only nine women! And the women were treated unfairly.

Some men at the law school didn't like having female students there. Women were even banned from one of the school's libraries. But that didn't stop Ginsburg. She got books from other places. She read a lot. She worked hard to become one of the best students in her class.

the Harvard Law School Library

Marty and Ruth play with their daughter, Jane, during a summer break from law school.

Life was very busy for Ginsburg. During the day, she went to classes. At night, she came home to take care of her daughter.

Then Marty got sick with cancer. Now Ginsburg needed to take care of him, too. He had to miss class to get medical care, so she took notes for him to study later. She asked their classmates to help him study. In time, he got better, and he graduated in 1958.

a graduation ceremony at Harvard University

Ginsburg's Cool Firsts

Ruth Bader Ginsburg was the first to do a lot of things. Did you know these firsts?

Ginsburg was the first Jewish woman to serve on the U.S. Supreme Court.

Ginsburg was the first person in her family to go to college.

Ginsburg was the first woman to become a tenured (TEN-yurd), or permanent, professor at Columbia Law School.

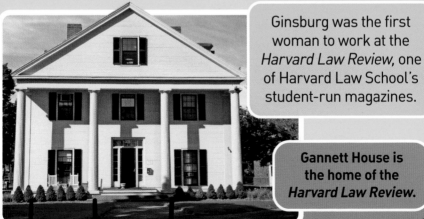

Ginsburg was the first woman to work at the *Harvard Law Review*, one of Harvard Law School's student-run magazines.

Gannett House is the home of the *Harvard Law Review*.

Back to the Big City

After Marty graduated from law school, he got a job as a lawyer in New York City. There was just one problem: Ginsburg still had one more year of law school.

Columbia University

Law school was important, but so was her family. She decided to leave Harvard to be with her husband and daughter.

Ginsburg finished law school at Columbia University in New York City. But then it was hard for her to find a job. Law firms didn't want to hire women as lawyers.

At first, Ginsburg took a job keeping records for a judge. In 1963, she got a job as a law professor at Rutgers University in New Jersey, U.S.A. She taught her students about the rules that courts have to follow. Two years later, Ginsburg's family grew when her son, James, was born. Now Ginsburg was raising two children while working full-time.

One day at Rutgers, a group of students asked Ginsburg to teach a class about the treatment of women under the law. Ginsburg liked this idea. She taught the students about the challenges women faced. This got her interested in working for women's equality.

Ginsburg taught law at Rutgers from 1963 to 1972.

Fighting for Equality

While at Rutgers, Ginsburg found out she was being paid less than male professors. She thought this was unfair. She joined other women at the school to demand equal pay. It worked!

Ginsburg leads a discussion at Columbia Law School.

CHEF SUPREME

Martin Ginsburg

That's a FACT! When Ginsburg worked late nights, her husband made dinner for the family. Years later, his favorite recipes were published in a cookbook.

In the late 1960s, women across New Jersey were reporting unfair treatment, too. Some didn't get equal pay, and others didn't have equal access to housing or health care. Ginsburg was asked to handle their cases.

Now Ginsburg wanted to do more to fight for equality. In 1972, she helped start the Women's Rights Project. That same year, she went back to Columbia University, this time as a professor. She worked as a lawyer for the project in addition to teaching.

Ginsburg led the Women's Rights Project from 1972 to 1980. It is still active today.

Through the Women's Rights Project, Ginsburg helped women get equal treatment under the law. She did this by bringing their cases to court.

When two people or groups disagree, they can go to court. Each side has a lawyer who explains the facts of the case. Then the judge, or sometimes a jury, decides which side is correct under the law. The judge tells the other side what they have to change.

In Her Own Words

"Fight for the things that you care about, but do it in a way that will lead others to join you."

Six of Ginsburg's cases were heard by the Supreme Court. Before each case, she listened to the stories of the people she was helping. She gathered information. Then she told the facts to the justices on the Court. The justices agreed with Ginsburg in five of her six cases.

In one case, a woman in the military wanted help paying for her home. Men in the military got help with housing. But they were given more money than she was given. Ginsburg said everyone in the military should be treated equally. The Court agreed, and the military changed its rules.

Ginsburg in 1977

In the Supreme Court chamber, the nine justices sit behind a raised wooden stand called a bench.

Beyond Women's Rights

Many of Ginsburg's cases were for women's rights, but she fought for men's rights, too. After one man's wife died, he needed money to take care of their child. He learned the government did not give men the same amount that it gave women in the same situation. Ginsburg argued his case—and won.

During this time, Ginsburg became a well-known lawyer. President Jimmy Carter heard of her work. In 1980, he asked

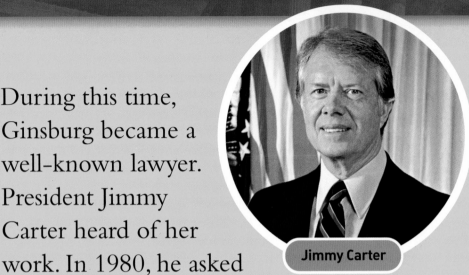

Jimmy Carter

Ginsburg to be a judge for the U.S. Court of Appeals for the District of Columbia.

In the federal court system, a district judge is the first to hear a case and make a decision. If people don't agree with the decision, they can take their case to a court of appeals. There, a new judge hears the case and makes a decision.

Words to Know

APPEAL: The act of taking a case to a higher court to be judged again

FEDERAL: Having to do with the national government

DISTRICT: Having to do with a specific area, such as a state or city

Types of Federal Courts

There are three types of federal courts: district courts, courts of appeals, and the Supreme Court. These courts hear cases between people from different states or cases that have to do with federal laws. A case can be brought to the next higher court on appeal.

U.S. District Court: There is at least one district court in every U.S. state—94 in total.

U.S. Court of Appeals: There are 12 courts of appeals. Each court hears cases for a different region of the United States.

Supreme Court: There is just one Supreme Court. It has the final say on any case that it hears.

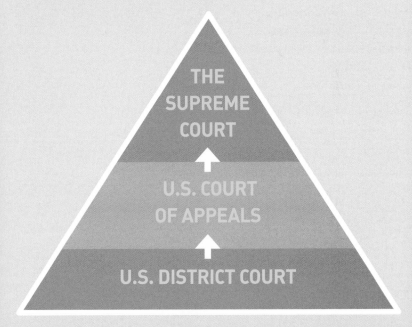

THE SUPREME COURT

U.S. COURT OF APPEALS

U.S. DISTRICT COURT

6 COOL FACTS
About Ginsburg

1 Ginsburg was a big opera fan. She even took part in performances with the Washington National Opera.

Growing up, Ginsburg was called Kiki by family and friends because she kicked a lot as a baby.

2

3 In 2019, Ginsburg won a million-dollar prize for her work on gender equality. She gave all the money to charities.

When she was a teenager, Ginsburg taught kids about the Jewish faith as a "camp rabbi" at a Jewish summer camp.

4

5

In high school, Ginsburg was a baton twirler and a cheerleader, and she played the cello.

At age 83, Ginsburg said she still did 20 push-ups every day.

6

Supreme Court

President Clinton walks with Ginsburg during her visit to the White House in Washington, D.C.

Ginsburg spent 13 years as a judge for the U.S. Court of Appeals. Then President Bill Clinton asked to meet with her. He was looking for a new justice for the Supreme Court. He already knew about Ginsburg's work for equality. He thought she would be a good justice.

Before Clinton could appoint Ginsburg, the U.S. Senate had to approve her. Ninety-six senators voted yes. Only three voted no. Ginsburg was sworn in on August 10, 1993.

Marty holds the Bible as Ginsburg is sworn in by Chief Justice William Rehnquist. President Clinton looks on.

Word to Know

APPOINT: To choose a person for a job or duty

As a Supreme Court justice, Ginsburg heard many important cases. One of these cases came in 2007. A woman named Lilly Ledbetter was working as a manager at a factory. She learned she was being paid less than the men doing the same job. She went to court to demand equal pay.

Lilly Ledbetter

The majority of justices decided against her case. They said she'd waited too long to bring it to court. Ginsburg dissented, or disagreed with the decision. But Ledbetter's fight didn't stop there.

That's a FACT! Ginsburg has been called "the great dissenter" for the strong statements she wrote when she disagreed with a Supreme Court decision.

Collar Code

Ginsburg often wore collars with her justice robes. She and former justice Sandra Day O'Connor started the tradition as a way to set themselves apart from the male justices, who wore ties. Ginsburg wore different collars for different events. Here's what some of them meant.

Majority: Ginsburg wore this gold collar when she agreed with the Court's decision.

Dissenting: When she disagreed with a decision, Ginsburg wore this now famous collar.

Everyday: This was one of Ginsburg's favorite collars.

Word to Know

MAJORITY: More than half of a total number

In her dissenting opinion on the Ledbetter case, Ginsburg said it was up to Congress to make a change. Some people in Congress agreed with Ginsburg. They worked to change the law to help women get fair pay.

In 2009, Congress passed the Lilly Ledbetter Fair Pay Act. It was the first bill signed into law by President Barack Obama. The new law changed the time limits for filing fair pay cases. Today it helps women in their fight for equal pay.

Word to Know

OPINION: A formal statement that explains why a decision was made

1933
Born in Brooklyn, New York, on March 15

1954
Graduates from Cornell University; marries Martin Ginsburg

1955
Gives birth to her daughter, Jane

President Obama signs the Lilly Ledbetter Fair Pay Act into law.

In Her Own Words

"Real change, enduring change, happens one step at a time."

1959
Graduates from Columbia Law School

1963
Begins teaching at Rutgers University Law School

1965
Gives birth to her son, James

Lasting Legacy

1972

Co-founds the Women's Rights Project; becomes a tenured professor at Columbia Law School

1973

Argues her first case in front of the U.S. Supreme Court

1980

Is appointed to the U.S. Court of Appeals

Ginsburg died on September 18, 2020. In her honor, all the U.S. flags outside federal buildings were flown at half-staff in the following days.

Both on and off the Supreme Court, Ginsburg raised her voice on cases that changed laws across the country. The changes she fought for will help people get fair treatment under the law for years to come.

1993
Is appointed to the U.S. Supreme Court

2007
Writes the dissenting opinion in the Lilly Ledbetter decision; Congress later passes the Lilly Ledbetter Fair Pay Act

2020
Dies on September 18, at age 87

QUIZ WHIZ

How much do you know about Ruth Bader Ginsburg? After reading this book, probably a lot! Take this quiz and find out. Answers are at the bottom of page 45.

1 Which president appointed Ginsburg to the Supreme Court?

A. Jimmy Carter
B. Barack Obama
C. John F. Kennedy
D. Bill Clinton

2 Where did Ginsburg get her first job as a law professor?

A. Harvard University
B. Columbia University
C. Rutgers University
D. Cornell University

3 In which city was Ginsburg born?

A. San Francisco
B. Brooklyn
C. Washington, D.C.
D. Atlanta

4

How many justices are on the Supreme Court?

A. three
B. five
C. six
D. nine

Ginsburg wore this collar when she _____.

A. agreed with a decision
B. disagreed with a decision
C. argued a case
D. heard a case

5

6

Growing up, Ginsburg saw prejudice against people who were _____.

A. Jewish
B. Christian
C. Buddhist
D. Hindu

What kind of musical performances did Ginsburg appear in?

A. jazz concerts
B. symphonies
C. operas
D. rock concerts

7

Glossary

APPEAL: The act of taking a case to a higher court to be judged again

EQUALITY: The same treatment and opportunities as others

FEDERAL: Having to do with the national government

PREJUDICE: A judgment or feeling of dislike about a person or group that is not based in fact

PROFESSOR: A teacher at a college or university

APPOINT: To choose a person for a job or duty

DISTRICT: Having to do with a specific area, such as a state or city

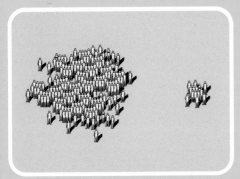

MAJORITY: More than half of a total number

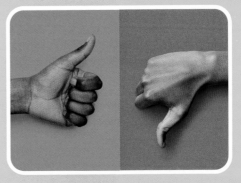

OPINION: A formal statement that explains why a decision was made

SCHOLARSHIP: Money given to a student by a school or group to help pay for the student's education

SUPREME COURT: The highest court of law in the United States

Index

Boldface indicates illustrations.

C
Carter, Jimmy 32, **32**
Clinton, Bill **36,** 36–37, **37**

E
Equality, fight for 6, 7, 24, 26–31, 34, 38, 40, **41,** 43

F
Federal courts 32, 33

G
Ginsburg, James 24
Ginsburg, Jane 14, **18**
Ginsburg, Marty 13–14, **14, 18,** 19, 22, 27
Ginsburg, Ruth Bader
    childhood 8–11, **34,** 34–35
    collar code 39, **39**
    college and law school **12,** 13–19, 21, 22–23
    cool facts 34–35, **34–35**
    cool firsts 20–21, **20–21**
    fight for equality 6, 24, 26–31, **28,** 34, 38, 40, 43
    Jewish heritage 8–9, 20, 35, **35**
    as judge 32, 36
    as lawyer 6, 27–32
    legacy 42–43
    marriage and children 14, **14, 18,** 22–23, 24
    as professor **7,** 21, **21,** 24–27, **25, 26**
    as Supreme Court justice **4,** 4–5, **6,** 20, **20,** 36–40, **37,** 39, **39, 42,** 43
    timeline 40–43
Glossary 46–47, **46–47**

H
Hitler, Adolf 9
Holocaust 9

J
Jewish people, prejudice against 8–9, **9**

L
Ledbetter, Lilly 38, **38,** 40, **41**

N
Nazis 9

O
Obama, Barack 40, **41**
O'Connor, Sandra Day 39

P
Prejudice
    against Jewish people 8–9, **9**
    against women 6, 16–17, 23, 26–30, 38, 40

R
Rehnquist, William **37**

S
Supreme Court 4–5, **4–5, 6,** 20, **20,** 30, **31,** 33, 36–40, **39, 42,** 43, 47, **47**

W
Women's rights 6, 16–17, 23, 24, 26–30, 38, 40, **41,** 42